Mel Bay's Children's Guitar Method

George Wright

By William Bay

1

HOW TO SELECT A GUITAR

When selecting a guitar for a child, it is essential that the instrument obtained is not too big for the student. In many cases, nylon strings will be easier for the student to begin on; however, many students do begin successfully on steel strings. For most children, I recommend a student size or a three quarter size guitar. In addition, you must make certain that the neck is not too wide. This is especially important if you are going to start the student on a nylon string guitar. Many nylon string guitars have very wide necks. Your local music shop can assist you on selecting the instrument. Be sure to take the student in and let the student hold the instrument to see if it is manageable. It is a good idea to check the strings to make certain that they are not too high off of the fingerboard at the nut, or first fret. (Consult the parts of the guitar diagram to see where this is.) Also, your teacher may help you check whether or not there are string buzzes on up the neck and whether or not the instrument plays in tune on up to about the 7th or 8th position. Most of the student model guitars being made today are of a very good quality and many of the problems which used to plague beginning guitarists are no longer concerns.

NOW AVAILABLE...A 60-minute video is now available which contains all the teaching content contained in this book. This video is highly recommended as a valuable learning aid and supplement to this guitar method. Also available are a split-track, play-along stereo cassette, and a compact disc.

THE GUITAR AND ITS PARTS

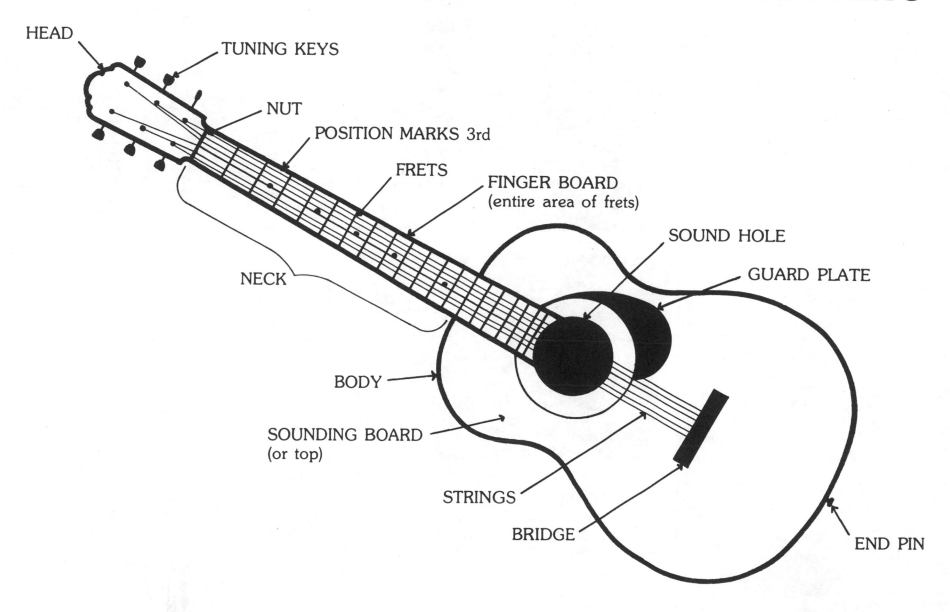

HOW TO HOLD THE GUITAR

Fig. 1

Fig. 2

Fig. 3

Fig. 4

Fig. 5

First, take hold of the guitar as shown in fig. 1. Next, bring it in close to the body as shown in fig. 2. Next, bring the right hand to the position shown in fig. 3. This is to bring the guitar firmly up against your body. The left hand is then moved, as shown in fig. 4, up into the area of first position. This is where the first finger is resting in the middle of the first fret. Finally, fig. 5 shows the right hand getting ready to strum the strings of the guitar.

STRUMMING THE STRINGS

Fig. 6

Fig. 7

At this point in the student's learning process we will be concentrating on coordinating chord fingering in the left hand with strumming motion in the right hand. We, therefore, recommend strumming with the thumb down across the strings. Later on we will introduce the possible use of a plectrum.

To strum the instrument, place the thumb by the sixth string. This is the largest of the six strings (figure 6). To strum down across the strings, bring the thumb down gently across all six strings. Do this a number of times until all of the strings sound at once. The strum should be even and the thumb should not rest too long on any one string. You should glide evenly across all six strings (figure 7).

The left hand should be positioned on the neck of the guitar so that the thumb rests comfortably in the middle of the back of the neck. This will require you to arch your hand somewhat. Look at the photos on page 5. By keeping the left-hand thumb in the middle of the neck, and by learning to play in this fashion from the beginning, your fingers will have the tendency to come down directly on top of the strings and avoid the problems of accidentally lying across the wrong string when you finger notes and chords.

LEFT HAND POSITION

When you lay your fingers across the wrong strings, you will accidentally deaden the sound of some of the notes. Proper positioning of the left hand will give you great freedom in fingering rapid passages later on. Also, by placing the thumb in the middle of the neck, you are providing maximum strength in fingering difficult chords.

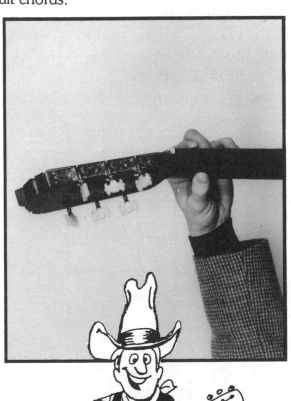

THE LEFT HAND

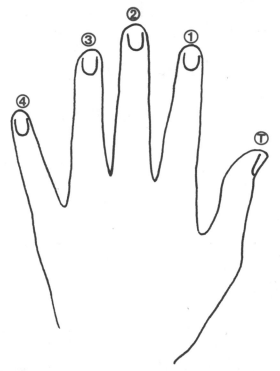

Numbers for the left hand fingers will appear in chord diagrams throughout the book.

TWO WAYS TO TUNE THE GUITAR

The six open strings of the guitar will be of the same pitch as the six notes shown in the illustration of the piano keyboard. Note that five of the strings are below the middle C of the piano keyboard.

1 | 2

1. Tune the 6th string in unison to the E or twelfth white key to the LEFT of MIDDLE C on the piano.

2. Place the finger behind the fifth fret of the 6th string. This will give you the tone or pitch of the 5th string. (A)

3. Place finger behind the fifth fret of the 5th string to get the pitch of the 4th string. (D)

4. Repeat same procedure to obtain the pitch of the 3rd string. (G)

5. Place finger behind the FOURTH FRET of the 3rd string to get the pitch of the 2nd string. (B)

6. Place finger behind the fifth fret of the 2nd string to get the pitch of the 1st string. (E)

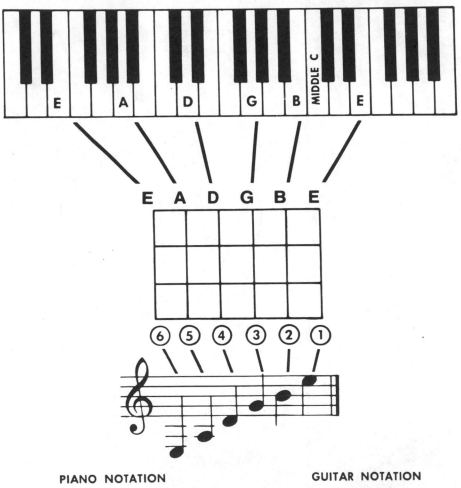

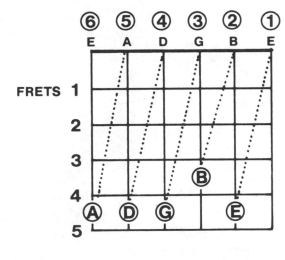

Pitch Pipes

Pitch pipes with instructions for their usage may be obtained at any music store. Each pipe will have the correct pitch of each guitar string and are recommended to be used when a piano is not available.

For more instruction on learning to tune your guitar - see Mel Bay's *Easy Way to Tune Guitar.*

PIANO NOTATION

E A D G B E

GUITAR NOTATION

STRINGS

6TH 5TH 4TH 3RD 2ND 1ST

E A D G B E

G CHORD - EASY FORM

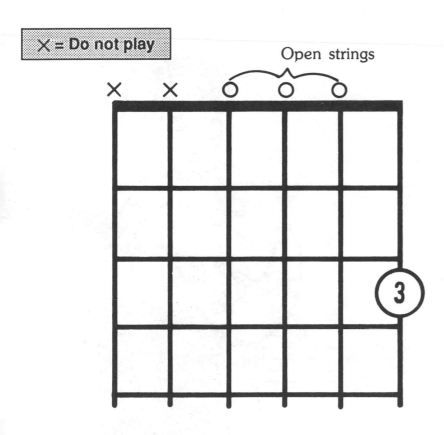

X = Do not play

Open strings

X = Do not play 6th & 5th strings
O = 4th, 3rd, & 2nd strings are played open
③ = Press the 3rd finger down on the 3rd fret on the 1st string

STRUMMING THE G CHORD

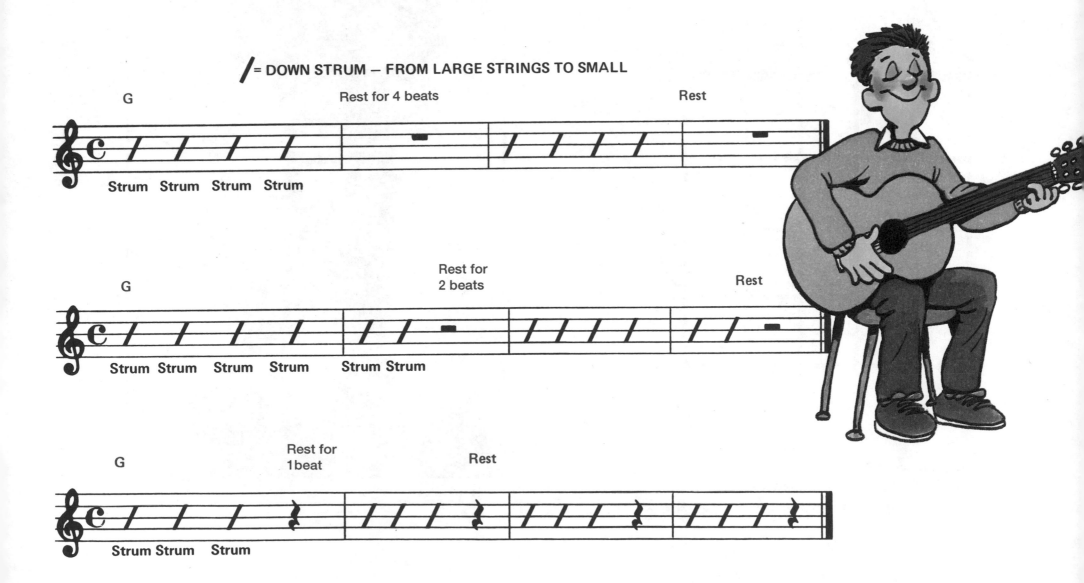

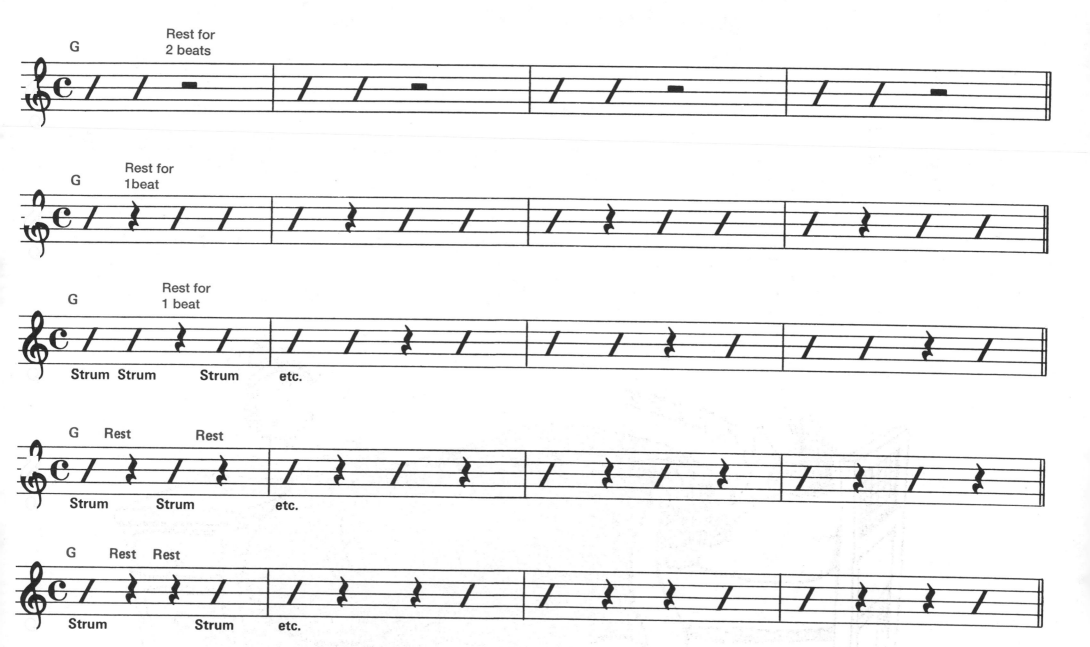

BROTHER JOHN SING & PLAY

C CHORD - EASY FORM

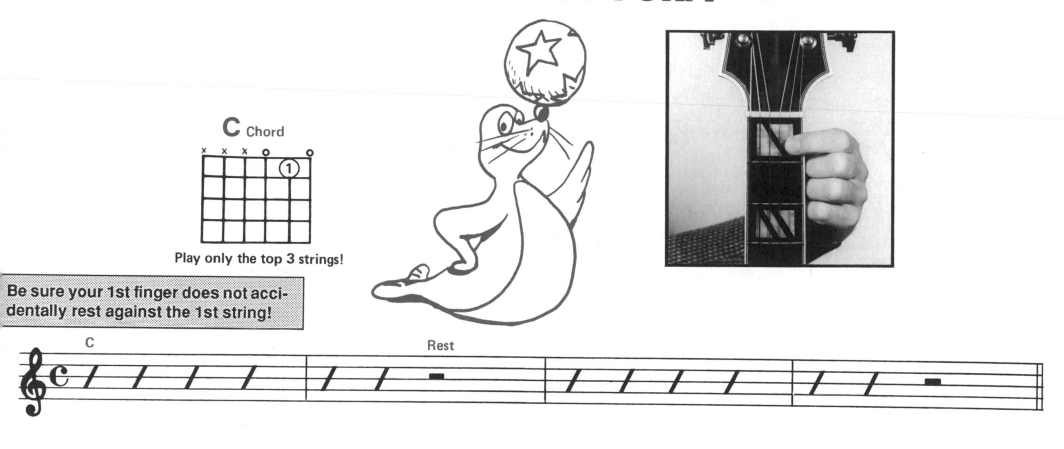

C Chord

Play only the top 3 strings!

Be sure your 1st finger does not accidentally rest against the 1st string!

THREE BLIND MICE - SING AND PLAY

ROW, ROW, ROW YOUR BOAT

G7 CHORD - EASY FORM

G7 Chord

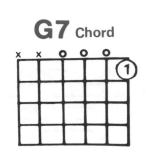

Play only the top 4 strings

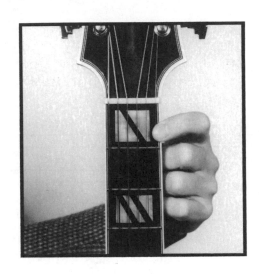

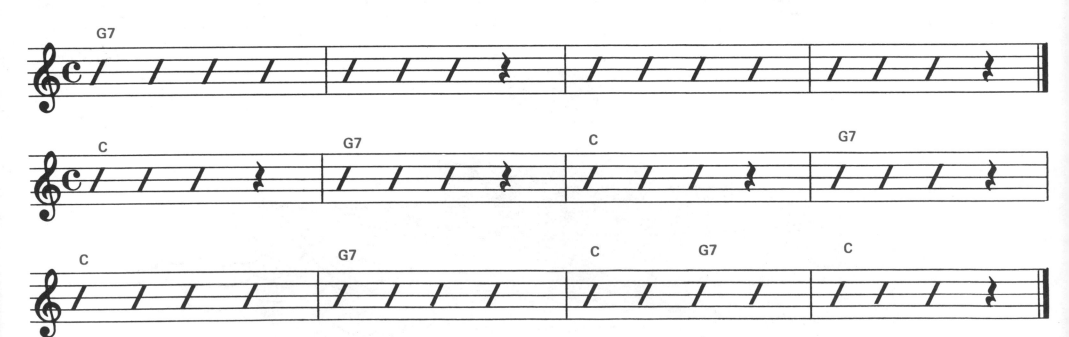

SKIP TO MY LOU

LONDON BRIDGE

C CHORD - ADD FOURTH STRING

C

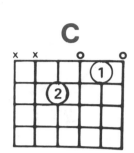

THIS OLD MAN

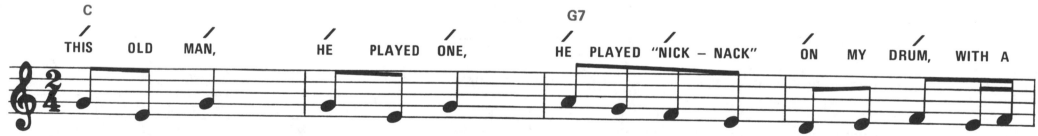

C — THIS OLD MAN,   HE PLAYED ONE,   G7 — HE PLAYED "NICK – NACK"   ON MY DRUM, WITH A

C — "NICK –NACK PAD – DY WHACK, GIVE MY DOG A BONE."   G7 — THIS OLD MAN CAME   ROLL – ING HOME. — C

3/4 TIME

Up till now, we have played either 4 strums per bar ($\frac{4}{4}$ or **C**) or 2 strums per bar ($\frac{2}{4}$).

Now we will play 3 strums per bar ($\frac{3}{4}$).

COWBOY'S SONG

Count 1 - 2 - 3, 1 - 2 - 3, etc.

Watch out for the rests!

POP GOES THE WEASEL

DOWN - UP STRUM

Up till now, we have only been strumming Down Across the strings.

Now we will strum Down and Up.

/ = DOWN STRUM   V = UP STRUM

HE'S GOT THE WHOLE WORLD

C

HE'S GOT THE WHOLE WORLD_____ IN HIS HANDS,_____ HE'S GOT THE

G7

WHOLE WORLD_____ IN HIS HANDS HE'S GOT THE WHOLE WORLD__ IN HIS HANDS,_ HE'S GOT THE

C

G7

WHOLE WORLD IN HIS HANDS._____

C

2. He's got the little bitsy baby. . . .

3. He's got you and me brother. . . .

BUFFALO GALS

THE FULL C CHORD

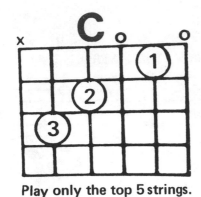

C

Play only the top 5 strings.

Try now to play the full C chord. Practise it until the notes all sound clean, being certain that your fingers are not accidentally touching the wrong strings.

TRY TO USE THE FULL C CHORD

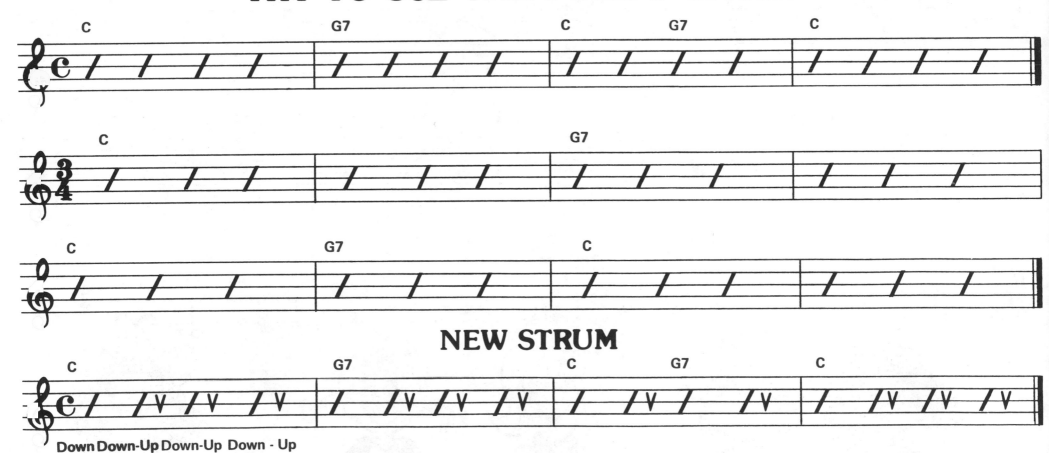

NEW STRUM

Down Down-Up Down-Up Down - Up

POLLY WOLLY DOODLE

HOLDING THE PLECTRUM

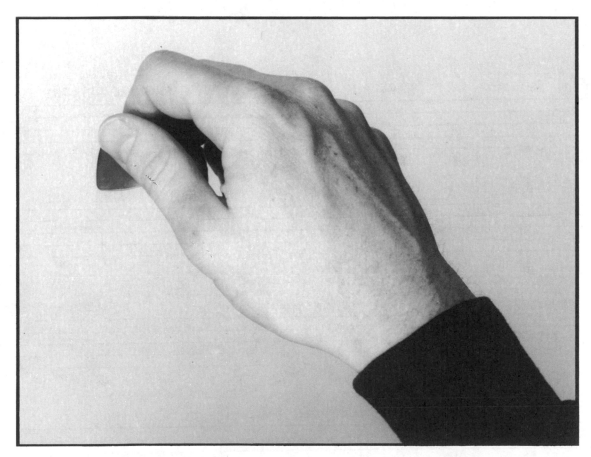

Now is the time to introduce the use of the flat plectrum. Study the photograph carefully, make certain that the plectrum is not held too tightly. Practise strumming up and down with the flat plectrum in order to get the feel of it. (The student may continue to use his thumb at this point if so desired by the teacher.) Make careful note of the symbols used to denote down stroke and up stroke. This will be used throughout as we learn to strum notes.

Check your hand position. Do not hold the plectrum too tightly!

⊓ = Down Stroke   V = Up Stroke

A WORD ABOUT STRUMMING

The following note-reading studies begin with alternate strumming. It is the author's belief that right-hand technique can best be developed by introducing the student to alternate strumming from the beginning. This enables the student to gradually increase the tempos on practise studies without having to change strumming technique to alternate strumming at a later date. All studies should begin at a slow tempo. By now the student should have some feeling for the down-up motion of the hand as a result of the chord strumming previously done. You will notice that all of the beginning studies utilizing note reading and alternate strumming require little or no string changes. The beginning studies do not even require fingering. Once the basic feeling for alternate strumming is established, the student's confidence and flexibility will progress rapidly and technique will be fluid.

The teacher may at this point, however, choose at his or her own discretion to begin the note-reading studies with all down strumming strokes. If this is the teacher's choice, then the author recommends the commencement of alternate strumming on page 26 when quavers are introduced.

LEARNING ABOUT NOTES

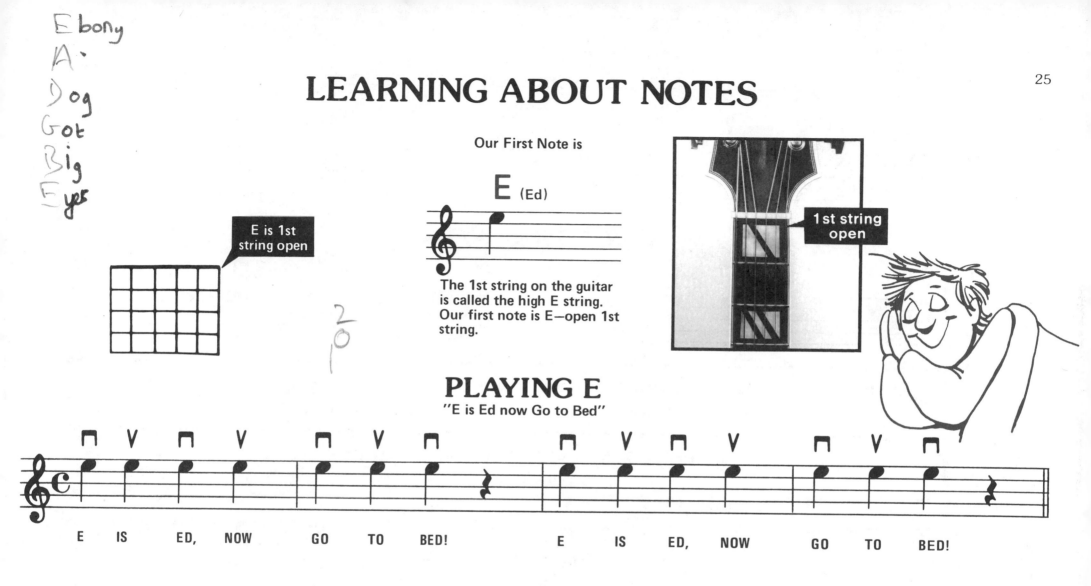

PLAYING E
"E is Ed now Go to Bed"

REST SONG

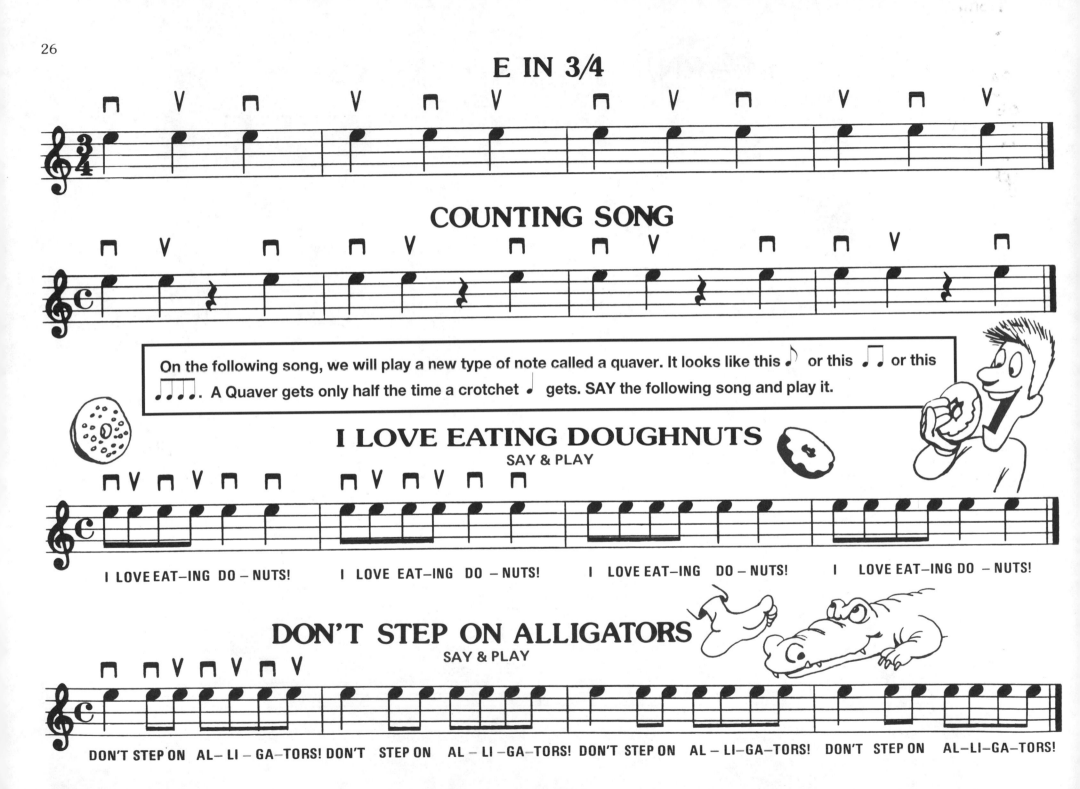

1st Fret 1st String

F (Fred)

F is 1st finger—1st Fret on the E string.

F IS FRED NOW SCRATCH YOUR HEAD

F IS FRED NOW SCRATCH YOUR HEAD. F IS FRED NOW SCRATCH YOUR HEAD.

EATING COOKIES MAKES ME HAPPY

SAY AND PLAY

EAT-ING COOK-IES MAKES ME HAP-PY, EAT-ING COOK-IES MAKES ME HAP-PY, EAT-ING COOK-IES MAKES ME HAP-PY, EAT-ING COOK- IES MAKES ME HAP-PY.

3rd Fret 1st String

G (Gail)

G is 3rd finger — 3rd Fret

G IS GAIL, GO STROKE A WHALE!

G IS GAIL, GO STROKE A WHALE! G IS GAIL, GO PET A WHALE!

WON'T YOU CLIMB THE STAIRS WITH ME

WON'T YOU CLIMB THE STAIRS WITH ME? CLIMB UP VER – Y CARE – FUL – LY.

CHASING RABBITS

CHAS – ING RAB – BITS ROUND THE LIL – Y MAKES THE PUP – PY ACT SO SIL – LY.

UP WE GO IN MY BALLOON

UP WE GO IN MY BAL – LOON I HOPE THAT WE'LL BE LAND – ING SOON!

SEE SAW

SEE SAW GO – ING UP AND DOWN, HOLD ON OR YOU WILL HIT THE GROUND!

B is the 2nd string

B (Benji)

The 2nd string open—is B

B is the 2nd string

B IS BENJI

BEN — JI   IS   THE   SEC — OND STRING, HE   REAL — LY   LIKES   TO   PLAY   AND   SING.

BENJI IS EATING CANDY

BEN—JI'S EAT—ING CAN — DY   HE JUST THINKS THAT'S DAN-DY.   BEN—JI'S EAT—ING   CAN — DY   HE JUST THINKS THAT'S DAN-DY.

BEE BUZZ

BEE—E   BEE—E   BUZZ BUZZ   BEE — E   BEE — E   BUZZ   BUZZ   BEE—E   BEE—E   BUZZ BUZZ   BEE—E   BEE—E   BUZZ BUZZ

E AND B STRING

CLIMBING

SURPRISE SONG

INDIAN DRUM

SAILING

WALKING OVER HILLS

TURKEY WALTZ

D7 CHORD

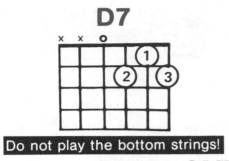

D7

Do not play the bottom strings!

PLAY ONLY THE TOP 4 STRINGS

Play slowly and make certain each note in the D7 chord sounds clear. Watch out for fingers accidentally resting on other strings and deadening the sound!

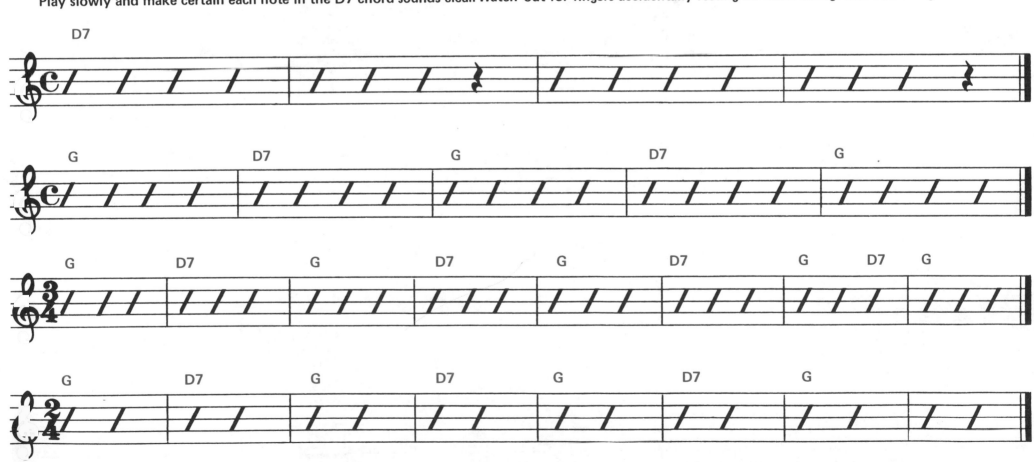

DOWN IN THE VALLEY
SING & PLAY

OH, MY DARLING CLEMENTINE

SING & PLAY

GO TELL IT ON THE MOUNTAIN

YANKEE DOODLE

SING & PLAY

LOOK OUT FOR THE C CHORD!

PRAISE HIM IN THE MORNING

AMAZING GRACE

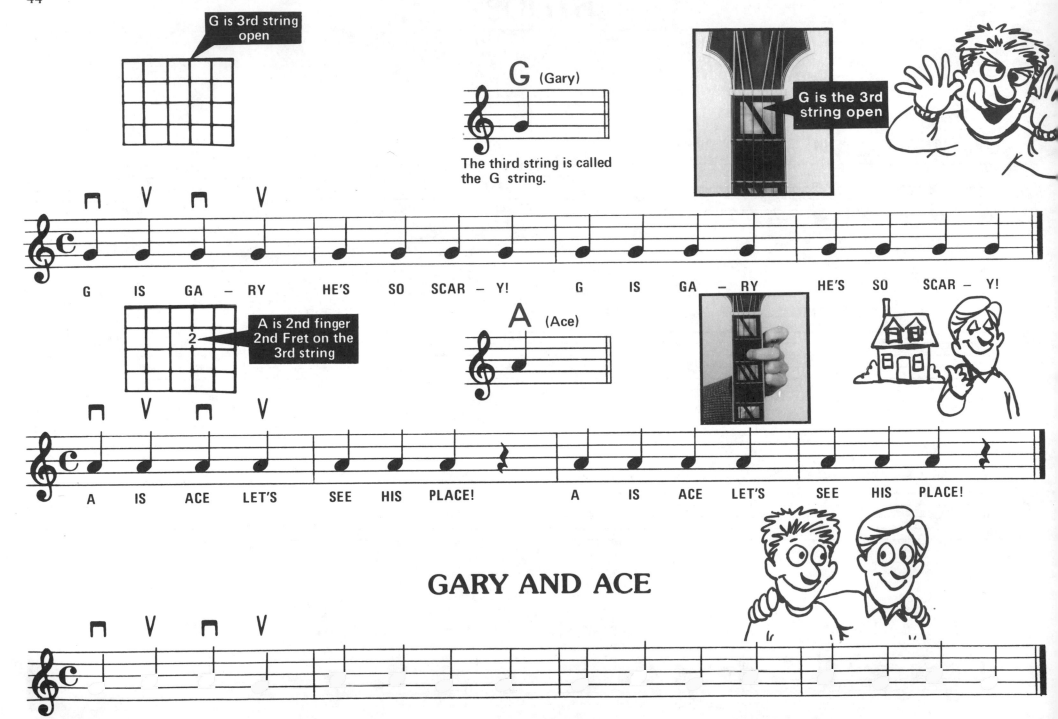

GARY AND ACE

STUDY

MINIM

This is a Minim ♩. It receives 2 counts.

AU CLAIR DE LA LUNE

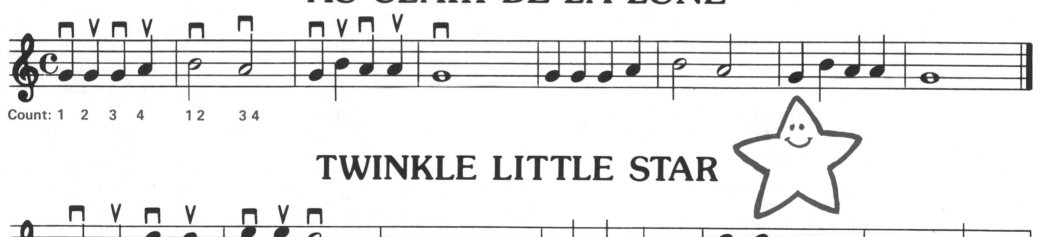

Count: 1 2 3 4 1 2 3 4

TWINKLE LITTLE STAR

JINGLE BELLS

THERE'S A HOLE IN THE BUCKET

YANKEE DOODLE SOLO

THE TIE

A tie looks like this ♩♩. It connects 2 or more notes. When you see a tie, pick the 1st note only.

RED RIVER VALLEY

SEMIBREVE

A semibreve looks like this ○. It gets 4 counts.

O WHEN THE SAINTS

Count: 1 2 3 4 1   1 2 3 4 1   1 2 3 4

1   1 2 3 4 1   1 2 3 4 1